"...
g...
s...
b... ... their feet, persuade the titans of industry to write huge checks to his campaign fund, or charm the panties off a long line of women – including his chief of staff. Sadly, he also misused that great gift in a vain attempt to hide the truth in court. Thanks to the Pulitzer Prize-winning reporting of Jim Schaefer and M. L. Elrick, he didn't get away with it. Now, Kwame's quotes are a lesson for all of us. A lie, beautifully told and passionately pronounced, is still a lie. Ultimately, the truth always wins. 'Hell yeah!' "

— HUEL PERKINS,
ANCHOR, FOX-2 DETROIT

"Kwame Kilpatrick rose to power on the strength of his words. It is sad that his words also paved his way to shame. No one tells his story better than he: the good, the bad and the awful. So don't let anyone else tell you. Let him. Experience the whole ride — in his own words."

**— ROCHELLE RILEY,
COLUMNIST, DETROIT FREE PRESS**

"The only thing you could trust Kwame to do is say something memorable ... a one-stop shop for all of Kwame's best BS."

**—DREW LANE, HOST OF THE TOP-RATED
DREW & MIKE SHOW, WRIF RADIO (101.1 FM)**

Oct. 17. He agrees to pay Brown and Nelthrope $8 million of taxpayer money, and pays Harris an additional $400,000 to settle his case, also dipping into the cash-strapped city's coffers for the funds. Kilpatrick says it is the right move for the city, his family and himself.

2008: The Free Press first reports on freep.com on Jan. 23 that text messages show Kilpatrick and Beatty lied under oath at the whistle-blower trial when they denied their affair and whether they intended to fire Brown. Wayne County Prosecutor Kym Worthy charges the pair with 15 felony counts on March 24. After fighting for months — and one day after historic removal hearings presided over by Gov. Jennifer Granholm begin — Kilpatrick pleads guilty to two counts of obstruction of justice and no contest to an assault charge stemming from an altercation with a sheriff's deputy. His resignation takes effect Sept. 18. After hours of last-minute legal wrangling, Kilpatrick is led off to jail on Oct. 28.

2009: With his normally close-cropped hair grown into a short afro, and sporting a thick beard, a slimmer and slightly dazed Kilpatrick is released on Feb. 3 after spending 99 days in a VIP cell at the Wayne County Jail. He says nothing as a phalanx of bodyguards hustle him into a waiting SUV. The next day he takes a charter flight paid for by his mother and joins his family, who have moved from Detroit to the tony Dallas-area suburb of Southlake. Within months, they move into a million-dollar home that is even larger than the Manoogian.

About the authors

Elrick and Schaefer hold up an early edition of
the Detroit Free Press at the Anchor Bar on the
day Kwame Kilpatrick entered a plea deal that
effectively brought the text message scandal
— and Kilpatrick's tenure as mayor — to an end.

"Kwame Kilpatrick was a brilliant politician and a fool, a lover and a hater, an inspiration to his race and a race-baiter, a liar and a thief, a man who thought he was serving God and a man who acted like he was God. But don't take my word for it. Take his."

— MICHAEL ROSENBERG, DETROIT FREE PRESS COLUMNIST AND AUTHOR OF "WAR AS THEY KNEW IT: WOODY HAYES, BO SCHEMBECHLER AND AMERICA IN A TIME OF UNREST"

"Chutzpah on a higher level. Falsely accusing me of buying prostitutes while he financed his own lurid love life with public dollars. It's all here, in his own words."

— STEVE WILSON, CHIEF INVESTIGATIVE REPORTER, WXYZ-TV (CHANNEL 7)

Acknowledgments

We would like to thank, first and foremost, our families for their love, courage, support and understanding while we were at the center of some of the craziest times in Detroit history.

This project would not have happened without the sage legal counsel of H. William Burdett Jr. and Eugene H. Boyle Jr. of Boyle Burdett, and David P. Sutherland of Wakefield Sutherland & Lubera, the business savvy of Mike Novak, Esq., the exquisite touch of Steve Dorsey, who designed the handsome volume you now hold, Brian Todd, our esteemed webmaster, and the keen eye of our chief copy editor, Alex Cruden. We also want to thank Drew Lane for his encouragement as well as our friends at the Wayne State University Press.

We cannot possibly heap enough praise on our colleagues at the Detroit Free Press. To list everyone at the paper to whom we owe a debt of gratitude would require a second volume... but since we're not yet sure how well this one will sell, they'll have to settle for a yard beer. That said, we must single out Steve Byrne. He knows why.

While we're at it, few reporters have had better legal representation than that provided by Herschel Fink and the firm Honigman Miller.

Jim Schaefer and M.L. Elrick stand with fellow reporter Bill McGraw in front of the FBI's 10 Most Wanted sign, right outside FBI headquarters in downtown Detroit.

We also want to salute those brave enough to stand up to Mayor Kilpatrick. Their stories were well documented in the Free Press and by our friends and competitors in the Detroit media, especially Darci McConnell, the first to smell something rotten in City Hall.

Lastly, we owe a tremendous debt to Bill McGraw, who inspires us still.

Presented by Watchmen Ink, LLC
Printed at Malloy Lithography, Ann Arbor, MI
ISBN # 978-0-615-33255-0
$7.99 per copy.
All contents ©2009

To order more please visit our website:
www.kwamesutra.com

Read the complete coverage of the Kilpatrick text
message scandal at **www.freep.com**

The Message Scandal

The text message scandal spelled the end of Kwame Kilpatrick's political career — at least for now.

In January 2008, the Detroit Free Press published excerpts from his messages with Christine Beatty, his chief of staff. The texts, nearly 14,000 of them typed out on city-issued pagers in 2002 and 2003, were anything but the usual order of business.

They showed, unequivocally, that the mayor and his chief of staff were lovers, and had also conspired to oust Gary Brown, a Detroit Police Department deputy chief in charge of internal affairs.

More than embarrassing, the text messages showed that Kilpatrick and Beatty had committed crimes. Just a few months earlier, both had testified in a civil trial that they were not intimately involved, and that they did not fire Brown. Brown and Harold Nelthrope, formerly one of the mayor's police bodyguards, had filed the suit alleging that Kilpatrick torpedoed their police careers to stop them from uncovering the mayor's philandering. Nelthrope's complaints to Brown's office of wild behavior by Kilpatrick and his police bodyguards had launched an internal affairs investigation. In the end, a jury awarded the ex-officers $6.5 million in damages.

Kilpatrick vowed to appeal the verdict, but a

month later made a surprising settlement with the former officers. The Free Press investigation proved why Kilpatrick did his about-face. The newspaper learned the former officers and their attorney had gotten hold of Kilpatrick's incriminating texts. His settlement with them — for $8 million in tax money — was not so much for the benefit of Detroit, as the mayor had said, as it was to benefit himself. The deal called for the ex-cops to hand over the text messages, and never speak of them again. The Free Press unearthed this secret settlement deal in a Freedom of Information Act lawsuit that Kilpatrick fought all the way to the Michigan Supreme Court.

Publication of the text messages showing Kilpatrick and Beatty lied under oath led to a combined 15 felony charges against them. They faced counts of perjury, obstruction of justice, conspiracy, and misconduct in office.

Beatty resigned a week after the Free Press published the text messages. But Kilpatrick hung on. He fought hard even after being charged criminally, vowing he would never quit on Detroit and — at times — attacking the media and the prosecutors. But in the summer Kilpatrick shoved a sheriff's deputy trying to serve a subpoena at the home of the mayor's sister. His fate was sealed. Calls for his resignation grew. And Gov. Jennifer Granholm fast-tracked historic public hearings to decide whether she should forcibly kick him out of office.

In September, on the morning of the governor's second hearing day, Kilpatrick finally buckled. He pleaded guilty to two counts of obstructing justice by committing perjury, and no contest to a third felony of assaulting the deputy. A judge sentenced Kilpatrick to 120 days in jail, forced him to surrender his law license, made him agree not to run for public office for five years and ordered him to repay $1 million to the City of Detroit. Beatty later pleaded guilty as well, and served 70 days of a 120-day sentence.

In February 2009, Kilpatrick emerged from his VIP cell in the Wayne County Jail after 99 days, his sentence lessened under state-mandated credits for good behavior. The next day, he boarded a private jet chartered by his mother and flew to Texas, where his wife and children were renting a home in the affluent suburb of Southlake, near Dallas. In June, while the former mayor argued in court pleadings that he was struggling to pay back more than $6 a month to the City of Detroit, he and his family moved to a gated community in Southlake — taking up residence in a million-dollar home more than 50 percent larger than Detroit's official mayoral residence, the Manoogian Mansion.

Parties, Strippers and Urban Legends

To date, rumors of a wild stripper party at the official mayoral residence haunt Kilpatrick. Though never proven, the rumor that he held a bacchanal gone-wrong when his wife arrived unannounced and assaulted a dancer played a significant role in shaping public perception of Kilpatrick. The lingering doubts were a constant source of frustration for him.

ON THE STEPS OF THE MANOOGIAN.
"I would never disrespect my God, my wife, my children or the citizens of Detroit with this nonsense."

AT THE MANOOGIAN, DENYING THE STRIPPER PARTY.
"It never happened. It never happened. It never happened."

ON PERCEPTIONS.
"When you're a 32-year-old with an earring in your ear, some people will believe that anything will happen."

COMPLAINING ABOUT THE MEDIA.
"This demonic influence has to stop. This frenzy has to stop."

AFTER THE ATTORNEY GENERAL RULED THERE WAS NO STRIPPER PARTY AT THE MANOOGIAN MANSION.

"Let's forget about the nonsense and let's go to work."

The Sensitive One

ON HIS FALL FROM GRACE.

"Three weeks ago ... I was on the cover of the front page of the Sunday paper. 'Best development person, managed the finances' and all this stuff. You find some text messages, now everything is wrong."

DISCUSSING THE IMPACT OF GARY BROWN'S WHISTLE-BLOWER LAWSUIT.

"If it wasn't for the Gary Brown situation, I probably would have had only three or four bad articles about me."

ON HIS MISSTEPS.

"I wish with all my heart that we could turn back the hands of time and tell that young man: Make better choices. But I can't."

AFTER HIS MOTHER AND FATHER WHIPPED UP THE CROWD AT HIS RE-ELECTION KICK-OFF IN 2005.

"I ain't cried since I was 10 years old."

TRYING TO DISPEL WHAT HE SAID IS A COMMON FEELING THAT HE'S "AN ENTITY."

"I'm a guy. I'm a dude. I'm a man. I'm a person."

RESPONDING TO A YOUNG MAN WHO ADDRESSED HIM AS "KWAME."

"It's Mr. Mayor. We ain't boys."

ON THE JOB OF MAYOR.

"This position is personal to me. It's much more than just politics. I want you to understand that."

AFTER HE BROUGHT DOWN THE HOUSE AT THE SYMPHONY, HIS PRESS SECRETARY TEXTED TO ASK WHETHER HE DANCED OR SANG.

"Fuck you nigga! LOL. I did a dramatic reading."

Oh, Really?

Kwame Kilpatrick made many sweeping statements that would leave Detroiters scratching their heads at his boldness – especially in hindsight.

ON WHY HE TOOK THE STAND IN THE WHISTLE-BLOWER TRIAL.

"I thought that the people of Detroit needed to have an opportunity to hear the truth, they needed to see me sit in the chair."

ON THE CHALLENGE OF LEADING DETROIT.

"The people of Detroit need to be convinced that Kwame Kilpatrick wakes up every day and all he does is work on their behalf, and he does that with integrity and character and honesty."

SAGE ADVICE FROM GRANDPA.

"My grandfather used to say that doing the same thing the same way over and over again and expecting a different result is the very definition of insanity."

ON WHETHER HE WOULD RESIGN, DURING THE TEXT MESSAGE SCANDAL.

"I feel bad for a lot of things that have happened, you know, mistakes. But you know some of them, even though the city had to go through them, they were things that were necessary to make me better."

TESTIFYING ABOUT WHETHER HE HOOKED UP WITH A JAMAICAN WOMAN IN A BARBER SHOP NEAR HIS BOYHOOD HOME.

"I played little league football in that neighborhood. My mother represented the neighborhood in the state legislature for 18 years. I represented that neighborhood in the state legislature for three terms. I'm now mayor. I know everyone ... the babysitter that I had watch me and my sister lives across the street, two houses over from that barbershop. That is my neighborhood. And so there was no occasion where I would be on the street with my wife and children and everybody that I know, with a Jamaican woman."

ON THE FUTURE OF HIS DEPOSED CHIEF OF STAFF, CHRISTINE BEATTY.

"After all is said and done she'll be recognized as one of the best people to ever serve in that position."

*PEOPLE ALWAYS WONDERED WHY HE DIDN'T
SETTLE THE POLICE WHISTLE-BLOWER
LAWSUIT THAT HELPED BRING HIM DOWN.*

"My own mother said settle."

*ASKED ABOUT THE SECRET SETTLEMENT
TO DEEP-SIX HIS TEXT MESSAGES.*

"There was no secret
deal; there was no
cover-up."

Man Of Few Words

ASKED UNDER OATH WHETHER HE AND CHRISTINE WERE ROMANTIC.

"No."

RESPONDING TO HIS WIFE'S TEXT ASKING HIM IF HE WAS READY FOR ROMANCE.

"Yepper!"

MAYORAL CALENDAR'S DESIGNATION FOR SECRET RENDEZVOUS WITH CHRISTINE.

"Gone fishin!!!"

RESPONDING TO CHRISTINE'S TEXT PROPOSAL: "WILL YOU MARRY ME?"

"Yes. When?"

Come Again?

*AFTER BEING CHARGED
WITH EIGHT FELONIES.*

"I look forward to complete exoneration."

SIX MONTHS LATER.

"I lied under oath."

---

*EXPRESSING OUTRAGE ON THE
WITNESS STAND ABOUT WHAT
HE DEEMED BLATANT CHAUVINISM.*

"It's absurd to assert that every woman that works with a man is a whore. I think it's disrespectful not just to Christine Beatty, but women who do a professional job every single day."

*IN A TEXT, AFTER CHRISTINE
INVITED HIM TO HER HOTEL ROOM.*

"Be there in 5 mins. Crack the door."

***RESPONDING TO ALLEGATIONS
BY FORMER MAYORAL BODYGUARDS
THAT HE WAS A PHILANDERER.***

"All of the allegations are completely false; it's a travesty that they would do that."

TEXTING CHRISTINE BEATTY.

"I've been dreaming all day about having you all to myself for 3 days. Relaxing, laughing, talking, sleeping and making love."

DEFENDING HIS HONOR.

"I don't whore around on my wife and I don't have wicked nude parties."

TEXTING CHRISTINE, HIS SOUL MATE.

"I thank GOD for allowing me to be your friend, lover and SM!"

JUSTIFYING HIS MANY OUT-OF-TOWN TRIPS.

"What we do there is try to get companies to come here. What we do there – in Washington, D.C., and New York, and in Atlanta and L.A., in Las Vegas — is try to get companies to locate in the city."

DAYDREAMING AND TEXTING CHRISTINE.

"I can't wait for Vegas. I want you uninterrupted to myself for a long time. If I can't have a lifetime, 2 days in Vegas is good. Love you!"

ON WHETHER A STRIP CLUB SHOULD OPEN DOWNTOWN.

"Entertainment is entertainment."

FIVE MONTHS LATER.

"I'm absolutely against any further development of any strip joints."

IN A 2002 TEXT TO CHRISTINE.

"Not 'til death do us part."

IN A 2008 INTERVIEW, AFTER SHE RESIGNED.

"We wish her well."

Kwame and The Media

TO HIS BODYGUARD, JUST BEFORE THE GUARD SLAMMED TV REPORTER STEVE WILSON INTO A WALL.

"Hold him, Mike."

TO JIM SCHAEFER, ONE OF THE FREE PRESS REPORTERS WHO FORCED KILPATRICK TO ADMIT THE CITY LEASED A LUXURY SUV FOR HIS WIFE – AS THE MAYOR PREPARED TO FACE HOSTILE REPORTERS:

"Jim, you gotta get 'em off me!"

***CRITICIZING A FREE PRESS
REPORTER, IN A TEXT.***

"Ben Schmidt is full of shit. This guy loves Gary Brown. He just made up this shit. This is soooo far from any truth. I know it won't stop. Just venting!"

***ON A CARD WITH FLOWERS TO RADIO HOST
MILDRED GADDIS, A RELENTLESS CRITIC,
AFTER HIS RE-ELECTION.***

"Have a nice day — Mayor Kwame Kilpatrick"

***IN A TEXT RESPONDING TO HIS PRESS
SECRETARY ABOUT THEN- COUNCILWOMAN
SHARON McPHAIL'S CALL FOR AN
ANTI-NEPOTISM RESOLUTION AND
A REQUEST FOR COMMENT FROM
THEN-REPORTER DARCI McCONNELL.***

"No response. Fuck her and Darci."

AT A RE-ELECTION RALLY, REGARDING TROUBLES OF HIS FIRST TERM.

"We're not stopping this progress because the news media are fixated on Kwame Kilpatrick."

ON REPORTERS WRITING ABOUT HIS BIG OUT-OF-TOWN TABS.

"Here we go again."

Mama's Boy

***TEXTING HIS MOTHER ABOUT THE
FALLOUT FROM GARY BROWN'S FIRING.***

"They are really trying to kick your son's butt! The media has launched an all out assault!"

ON EARLY BEGINNINGS.

"I started in politics when I was 5 years old, because my mother pulled out a belt and said, 'You're going to knock on these doors.' It was fun then; it's fun now."

***ON EMULATING THE LOOK
OF HIP-HOP STARS.***

"Until my mother kind of slapped me and said, 'Hey, put on a suit.'"

*AFTER HIS MOTHER BREAKS THE NEWS THAT
HE WILL NOT BE PERMITTED TO ACCOMPANY
HER ON A CONGRESSIONAL TRIP TO NIGERIA.*
"Try for me. Ask the Prez!"

Kwame and The D

AFTER WINNING RE-ELECTION.
"Detroit voters are very smart.
Matter of fact, they are brilliant.
Not just because they voted for
Kwame Kilpatrick."

*UNINTENTIONALLY IRONIC THEME
OF HIS 2006 INAUGURAL.*
"Detroit Love."

ON THE IMPACT OF HIS ACTIONS.
"I carry this city in my soul …
so when I hurt people and
disappoint people, I take it
personally."

URGING PERSONAL RESPONSIBILITY, 2007 STATE OF THE CITY SPEECH.

"My beloved community, I truly understand the history of African-American people in this country. ... But we have come to a point in our community where there is no outside conspiracy doing this to us. This is us killing us. ... And we, as a community, have to stop it now. Nobody's coming to save us."

DISCUSSING CALLS FOR HIS RESIGNATION.

"I wear the city on my back, on my shoulders, my chest, my head. I'm a Detroiter through and through. You know, Detroiters sometimes, they love to hate, but they also give me love, so that's who I am."

EXPLAINING WHY HE DITCHES HIS BODYGUARDS TO TAKE LATE-NIGHT DRIVES ALONE.

"I roll down the windows and have time with Kwame in Detroit."

SOLO DRIVES II.

"I like being with the city by myself, because this is the city that gave me so much."

ON HATERS.

"I think that Detroit oftentimes is enamored with killing itself. We circle the wagons and shoot in."

ON HATERS II.

"We have not had a mayor in my lifetime that hasn't been humiliated, degraded, attacked by the community and the media."

*AFTER DECLARING DETROIT
"GOD'S CITY" DURING HIS FIRST
PUBLIC APPEARANCE AS MAYOR.*

"There's some places you can go in this country where they say you're crazy for loving this city. If I'm wrong, I don't want to be right."

*TELLING SUPPORTERS WHY HE
THOUGHT THEY STUCK WITH
HIM DURING HIS RE-ELECTION BID.*

"Some of y'all just plain crazy."

Mister Misunderstood

ON STEREOTYPES.

"When you're a young African-American mayor with an earring in your ear, it's kind of hard for people to believe you're a good dad and husband."

ON THE DAY THE FREE PRESS REPORTED THAT HIS STEP-BROTHER HAD A CRIMINAL RECORD, INCLUDING DOMESTIC VIOLENCE CHARGES.

"I never got in trouble my entire life, never, until I got this job."

AT HIS PLEA HEARING, ON THE RIGHT TO BE PRESUMED INNOCENT.

"I gave that up a long time ago, your honor."

Kwame
on Fitness

REFUTING MEN'S FITNESS MAGAZINE'S
DESIGNATION OF DETROIT AS
"THE FATTEST CITY IN AMERICA."

"I'm not sure I agree with their criteria. But it didn't help much when I showed up on television."

ON THE DETROIT FREE PRESS MARATHON.

"When I hear the word marathon, I go the other way."

The Philosopher King

RESPONDING WITH SARCASM TO PROBLEMS THAT PREDATED HIS TERM.

"I'm the mayor, so it's my fault."

ON BEING BOLD.

"If you're going to make a mistake, make an aggressive mistake."

A MOMENT OF CANDOR, EARLY ON IN THE TEXT MESSAGE SCANDAL.

"I hope I served as an example of 2002 to 2008 of what not to do. Because you've got to learn from not only your own mistakes, but the mistakes of others. And I made plenty."

IN A TEXT TO FRIEND BOBBY FERGUSON, EXPLAINING HIS SPIRITED PUBLIC RESPONSE TO ALLEGATIONS SWIRLING AROUND GARY BROWN'S FIRING.

"This is politics and PR. People want to see their mayor be a leader, make a strong affirmative stmt, then shut up. ... I was confident and calm. I believe there has to be one comment of disgust and indignation. Women (70% of voters) loved that shit. Young men always have a fuck them niggas attitude. I choose women. Fight for family, children."

AFTER SURVIVING HIS FIRST TERM.

"I want to be a great man. ... I want to be a great mayor. I believe I was chosen to do this."

AT THE FUNERAL FOR CIVIL RIGHTS ICON ROSA PARKS.

"Thank you for sacrificing for us. Thank you for praying when we were too cool and too cute to pray for ourselves. ... Thank you for allowing us to step on your mighty shoulders."

Kwame & Friends

DISMISSING CONCERNS ABOUT BEING A PUPPET OF WAYNE COUNTY EXECUTIVE ED McNAMARA.

"I'm too big to fit in Ed McNamara's pocket."

WRITING TO A JUDGE SEEKING LENIENCY FOR A PUBLIC OFFICIAL CONVICTED OF HIDING CASH FOR A VIOLENT GANG.

"I believe Mr. Stallworth to be a highly ethical and spiritual individual with a profound love of family, deep commitment to his community and a firm believer that one individual can affect change."

*DESCRIBING BEST FRIEND BOBBY FERGUSON,
WHO WAS CHARGED (LATER CONVICTED) IN
AN EMPLOYEE'S PISTOL-WHIPPING.*

"A dedicated family man and one of the hardest working people I know. He is a dynamic businessman who is committed to Detroit and has a long-standing record of service in our city."

*QUOTED BY A FEMALE COP, WHO TESTIFIED
THAT KILPATRICK SUGGESTED SHE HAVE
SEX WITH HIS PAL BOBBY FERGUSON.*

"Take care of my boy."

Football Is Life

"I hit people. And I hit them pretty hard. And I enjoyed it. Therefore, they gave me a college scholarship. No one would accept me on my grades or my test scores."

OUTLINING HIS RE-ELECTION STRATEGY.

"It's time for some offense. As an offensive tackle, I can't wait to hit someone."

Simply Divine

Kwame Kilpatrick claimed he decided to run for mayor after he meditated in the basement of his home, opened up a Bible and stumbled upon a passage wherein David took control of Judah at age 30 – Kilpatrick's age at the time. He went on to invoke the Heavenly Father often throughout his six-year reign.

ON SIGNS FROM ABOVE.
"I believe I'm on an assignment from God."

KILPATRICK'S PRESCRIPTION FOR A CITY RAVAGED BY VIOLENCE.
"We need a spiritual movement."

ON HIS COMMITMENT TO THE JOB.
"I believe something bad would happen to me if I walked away from this blessing."

DURING THE TEXT MESSAGE
SCANDAL, ON CROSSING GOD.

"A lot of people are saying this is the devil doing this to me. I want to be clear that this is not the devil doing this to me. God allowed this to happen in my life because there are certain things that I've done that have been disobedient."

AFTER SETTLING THE
WHISTLE-BLOWER SUIT.

"I will dedicate my life to transforming Detroit into the city we all know it can become and that God intended for it to be."

Kwame Style

ON HOW HIS PREDECESSOR
DECORATED THE OFFICE.

"This is not my style. You know me better than that."

ON RUMORS OF WILD BEHAVIOR.

"I think the reason that it comes out is that we are sexy. I think this is a sexy administration."

IN A 2001 VOICEMAIL MESSAGE LEFT
FOR ATTORNEY GEOFFREY FIEGER.

"Geoff Fieger, how you doing? I hope everything's going well for you. I'm sure it is. Every time I turn on the television, you're making more money. I need some of it now. I need your support and your help in this campaign."

Sweet Nothings

Kilpatrick and Christine Beatty became close friends at Cass Tech High School in Detroit. After graduation in 1988, their relationship continued on both a personal and professional level and – after Kilpatrick took office in 2002 – their text messages show their relationship had become intimate. Beatty was both Kilpatrick's lover and, as his chief of staff, his most trusted adviser.

IN A TEXT TO CHRISTINE.

"You were my girl for as long as I can remember. I was too young and stupid to know. I promise for the rest of my life you will be my girl."

TEXTING FOR A RENDEZVOUS WITH CHRISTINE.

"I need you soooo bad."

TO THE LOVE OF HIS LIFE, IN A TEXT.

"I really knew I would be with you since 12th Grade. Just a matter of time."

AFFIRMATION, IN A TEXT.

"Remember, I love you with all my heart, mind and soul. You complete me. I will not allow you to fall. Ever!"

TEXTUAL LOVE, IN MANY WAYS.

"I do express how much I love you everyday. Sometimes that expression comes in the form of worry, irritability, stress or even anger. But is all because of love. Loving you is constant."

TEXTING CHRISTINE.

"I'm madly in love with you."

**CHEERING UP HIS CHIEF OF
STAFF — OR COS — IN A TEXT.**

"You are a star. You are brilliant.
There would be no Mayor
Kilpatrick w/o you. You are
the best COS to ever be in city
gov't."

TRUST IN THE LORD, IN A TEXT.

"Rest your mind! God has got
your back. You have come too
far. And you are one of his
favorites. Trust him!"

Casanova Kwame

He was married to Carlita, in love with Christine and swore his loyalty to both. But his text messages show Kilpatrick juggled several other women at the same time.

IN A TEXT, CHRISTINE WONDERED WHAT HE WOULD THINK IF SHE RAN INTO HIS ARMS AND GAVE HIM A ROMANTIC KISS IN PUBLIC.

"Wouldn't be wrong. Just would send shockwave through city, state, county. LOL."

IN A TEXT TO ANOTHER GIRLFRIEND.

"I was about to jump your bones in Ford Field! LOL."

TEXTING YET ANOTHER GIRLFRIEND.

"Can't get you out of my system! Don't want to either. Have a wonderful day."

TEXTING STILL ANOTHER GIRLFRIEND.
"My d*** needs to be sucked. It's been a while. I missed your ass today at Belle Isle."

WAIT, THERE'S ANOTHER GIRLFRIEND.
"I want some (name withheld) time."

TEXTING HIS RESPONSE TO AN INVITATION TO WATCH TWO WOMEN.
"Put it together!"

QUOTED BY A POLICE BODYGUARD, WHO SAID KILPATRICK WANTED HIM TO CHECK OUT THE WOMEN AT A WASHINGTON, D.C., NIGHTCLUB.
"Man, you're going to see some bad hammers."

Master of Understatement

ADMITTING AFTER WEEKS OF DENIALS THAT THE CITY LEASED A LUXURY LINCOLN NAVIGATOR FOR HIS WIFE.

"There were some screw-ups on communications."

ON THE MISTAKES OF HIS FIRST TERM.

"As mayor of Detroit, I realize at times I have been an imperfect servant."

SHORTLY AFTER THE TEXT MESSAGE SCANDAL BROKE.

"There have been times that I wasn't thinking too well."

Master of Overstatement

*AFTER A FAVORABLE RULING
IN HIS PERJURY CASE.*

"When you really think about it, from 1776 to 2008, men, women of all ages, colors and creeds died in this country for Kwame Kilpatrick and you have to have the right to a fair trial. So it's not about the politics as much as it is about the American jurisprudence system that we can't allow to be bastardized."

*EXPRESSING CONFIDENCE AS HE
FACED EIGHT FELONY CHARGES.*

"I think the prosecutor's case is going to hell quickly."

*TWO DAYS AFTER HE LOST
THE WHISTLE-BLOWER CASE.*

"My people were hung from trees. If they can go through that, then I can definitely stand up and wake up in the morning, kiss my babies and go to work."

LASHING OUT AT THE MEDIA.

"We've never been in a situation like this before, where you can say anything, do anything, have no facts, no research, no nothing."

Master of Misdirection

DENYING ON THE WITNESS STAND THAT HE WAS ROMANTICALLY INVOLVED WITH LOU BEATTY'S WIFE.

"Lou Beatty grew up three houses down from me. We played on the same Little League team. He played football with me, yes, at Cass Tech. He's out there, at 6 o'clock he'll be coaching my sons tonight."

ON RUMORS OF WILD BEHAVIOR.

"A lot of people who disagree with decisions we are making in city government, they start rumors as a form of offense, or defense. But it's all garbage. Incredible garbage."

Family Matters

PLAYFULLY WARNING DETROITERS AT HIS 2002 INAUGURATION NOT TO MESS WITH HIS LARGE FAMILY.

"Don't start none, won't be none."

ON DIVORCE, IN A TEXT TO CHRISTINE.

"My parents divorced when I was 10 yrs old. I thank God for them. They were better for me, Yann, Diarra, because of it. I REALLY don't remember them together. Just faint memories."

TEXTING CHRISTINE, WHO WANTED TO KNOW WHAT HIS WIFE OFFERS THAT SHE DOESN'T.

"The tremendous bond of parenthood. J, J & J's mama. The Birth Experiences and the Dreams for our children."

*RESPONDING TO CHRISTINE'S TEXT ASKING
IF HIS KIDS SEE THEIR PARENTS AS UNHAPPY.*

"They absolutely don't see that.
Nobody does! We are real good
at masking that shit. Plus I do
a lot of stuff with the family.
I know if I ever made the big
decision, my kids would be fine.
EVENTUALLY!"

*HOURS BEFORE REPORTERS REVEALED THAT
HIS STEP-BROTHER HAD BEEN CONVICTED OF
ASSAULTING HIS LIVE-IN GIRLFRIEND TWO
YEARS EARLIER.*

"I have never come in contact
with anybody in the criminal
justice process, neither me or
my family."

ON KEEPING HIS TWIN BOYS AWAY FROM GAYS.

"I don't want Jelani and Jalil out there, you know, even seeing that type of lifestyle."

AFTER A BACKLASH.

"I didn't realize I was speaking into such a large microphone."

EXPLAINING HIS MIDDLE NAME, IN A TEXT.

"Malik means King or Leader. My dad just liked it."

AFFIRMING HIS COMMITMENT.

"I don't whore around on my wife. ... I want people to understand that I would never disrespect my God, my wife or my children."

IN A WRITTEN STATEMENT TO THE FREE PRESS, MINUTES BEFORE PUBLICATION OF THE TEXT MESSAGE INVESTIGATION.

"These five- and six-year-old text messages reflect a very difficult period in my personal life. It is profoundly embarrassing to have these extremely private messages now displayed in such a public manner. My wife and I worked our way through these intensely personal issues years ago. I would now ask that the public and the media respect the privacy of my wife and children and of Christine Beatty and her children at this deeply painful moment for our families."

***ON TELLING HIS SONS
ABOUT HIS INFIDELITY.***

"For the first time in my life, I had to have a conversation with my 12-year-old twin sons about very grown-up things. It was, without a doubt, the hardest conversation I've ever had in my entire life."

***DEPUTY BRIAN WHITE ON
KILPATRICK'S REACTION WHEN
WHITE BROUGHT A SUBPOENA
TO THE MAYOR'S SISTER'S HOUSE.***

" 'Get the fuck out of here. Leave my fucking family alone. Get off my fucking porch.' "

It's Good to be King

IN A TEXT TO CHRISTINE.

"Just landed.
I Love this private
plane shit. LOVE IT."

TEXTING CHRISTINE ABOUT A POLICE
BODYGUARD HE WANTS TRANSFERRED OUT.

"I'm on my way to Lions facility.
When I finish working out the
MF better be gone."

TO THOUSANDS OF JEERING RED WINGS
FANS CELEBRATING THE STANLEY CUP.

"The beer's on me!"

Kwame and Race

He came into office urging racial harmony, but a few of his public statements — and several of his text messages — show he wasn't above seeing things in black and white.

CALLING MICHIGAN AN ULTRA-CONSERVATIVE STATE WITH AN ANTI-DETROIT LEGISLATURE.

"This is the Mississippi of the North."

BLAMING THE MEDIA FOR HIS TEXT MESSAGE TROUBLE.

"This unethical, illegal, lynch mob mentality has to stop."

TEXTING CHRISTINE ABOUT IGNORING HER CRITICS.

"I really love you! Focus on the strategy. White men will never define you the way you want. They WILL respect you! Strategy!"

**TEXTING CHRISTINE ABOUT NOT
GOING TOGETHER TO AN EVENT.**

"LOL. Nope. Too many white people! Too many questions."

**ON MACKINAC ISLAND, AFTER A SUBURBAN
POLITICIAN BROUGHT UP CRIME IN DETROIT.**

"What is it with you white people? ... You love your drug wars. We don't have a drug war going on."

**ON ALLEGED HARASSMENT DURING THE
TEXT MESSAGE SCANDAL, AT THE 2008
STATE OF THE CITY ADDRESS.**

"In the past 30 days I've been called a nigger more than any time in my entire life."

PROSECUTOR'S INVESTIGATOR JOANN KINNEY ON KILPATRICK'S REACTION WHEN SHE TRIED TO SERVE A SUBPOENA WITH DEPUTY BRIAN WHITE.

" 'You, a black woman, being with a man last name White, you should be ashamed of yourself and ... why are you a part of this?' "

ON PROSECUTOR KYM WORTHY'S MOTIVES.

"Her hope is that the racism of this region will convict me instead of the issues of the law and justice."

COMPLAINING THAT RACE PLAYED A ROLE IN THE SPREAD OF THE MANOOGIAN STRIPPER PARTY RUMOR.

"It would never be done to a white politician."

***VENTING DURING THE TEXT
MESSAGE SCANDAL.***

"All of a sudden, you just get
corrupt, ignorant, stupid, lazy
and promiscuous. And I just
think that this is a reality check
— not just on Kwame Kilpatrick,
because, you know, I'm God's
guy; I'm going to be all right —
I think this is for all black men
right now in the city of Detroit."

Politically Speaking

ADDRESSING HIS YOUTHFULNESS WHEN HE KICKED OFF HIS MAYORAL CAMPAIGN.

"People have said, 'You'll be great eight years from now, 12 years from now. ... That mentality has kept us in degradation for too long. We don't have eight years. We need to stop wasting time."

TEXTING CHRISTINE ABOUT COUNCILWOMAN SHEILA COCKREL.

"Why is Sheila always looking for a scandal with us? That bitch ain't right!"

*KIDDING A SPEAKER ABOUT WHAT
WOULD HAPPEN IF HE SKIPPED STATE
SEN. MARTHA G. SCOTT'S MIDDLE INITIAL
IN HER INTRODUCTION.*

"Forget the 'G' and
she'll cut you."

*ON A COUNCILWOMAN WHO CALLED HIM A
THUG AND SAID HE TRIED TO ELECTROCUTE
HER BY WIRING HER DESK CHAIR.*

"I think that the people who care
about Sharon McPhail, and who
love her, we all really need to
wrap our arms around her. She
really needs some help."

Oh, Really? (Part II)

FIGHTING BACK DURING THE TEXT MESSAGE SCANDAL.

"I think we're going to be completely vindicated politically, completely vindicated legally."

TELLING A JUDGE ABOUT LESSONS LEARNED AFTER CRIMINAL CHARGES.

"My life has been revolutionarily transformed."

RESPONDING TO WASHINGTON, D.C., POLICE COMPLAINING THAT HE PARTIED TOO HARD IN THEIR TOWN.

"It's not true that I go nightclubbing. I don't do that here or anywhere."

IN A TEXT, CHRISTINE BEATTY ASKED HIM TO DIVULGE SOMETHING SHE DIDN'T KNOW.

"OK, I sold weed in college!"

*ON HIS GRANDIOSE PLAN TO TRANSFORM
THE ABANDONED DOWNTOWN TRAIN
STATION INTO A STATE-OF-THE-ART
POLICE HEADQUARTERS.*

"We want it to be a symbol of
our renaissance, of our rebirth,
of our resurgence."

Come Again?
(Part II)

*2007 TESTIMONY ABOUT TAKING
ACTION AGAINST GARY BROWN.*

"It wasn't to hurt him, step on
him, do things to him. And I
think my remarks and different
things that I've said from the
time it happened, even under all
the adversity and pressure, have
been respectful to that degree."

*2003, IN A TEXT AFTER BROWN'S
TELEVISED PRESS CONFERENCE.*

"I just saw ch. 4. ...
We got to get his ass."

***A VOW TO FIGHT, IN A PRESS CONFERENCE
AFTER LOSING THE WHISTLE-BLOWER TRIAL.***

"Obviously, from a business perspective, we don't have the money to settle ... we don't believe that we should pay this verdict, and we don't believe that absolutely in law that there's any significant facts that gives a basis for them to have these dollars."

ONE MONTH LATER.

"Since the verdict, I've listened to pastors, business leaders and so many Detroiters who genuinely love and care about me and this city. ... I've humbly concluded that a settlement ... is the correct decision for my family and the entire Detroit community."

TESTIFYING ABOUT TERMINATING
GARY BROWN, 2007.

"I know it was the right decision.
I knew it then, I know it now."

TEXT MESSAGE, 2003.

"We must answer the question?
Why was Gary Brown fired. ...
It will be asked, I need short,
powerful answer ... I just need a
good answer whatever it might
be."

ON LAWSUIT ALLEGATIONS BY
FORMER MAYORAL BODYGUARDS
THAT HE IS A PHILANDERER.

"They will say anything to get
money."

TEXTING CHRISTINE, WHO WAS WORRIED
THAT BODYGUARDS HEARD THEIR
LOVEMAKING IN A HOTEL.

"Damn that. Never busted.
Busted is what you see!"

JANUARY 2008 TELEVISION ADDRESS.

"I would never quit on you. Ever."

NINE MONTHS LATER.

"Sometimes standing strong means stepping down."

Kwame at the Helm

UPON TAKING OFFICE.
"It's time for all of us to rise up and start our future – right here, right now!"

ON BETTER GOVERNMENT.
"The city of Detroit is not a poor city, it's a woefully mismanaged city."

ON WHO KWAME KILPATRICK IS.
"I'm your grandson. I'm that little boy you told to stay off the grass. I'm also the little boy you told to stay in school, to get a good education, to love and serve God and to be responsible to others and, after that, to come back and serve the community."

ON THE CAMPAIGN TRAIL.

"We don't have four more years to start our future. We don't have eight more years to start our future. Our future has to begin, right here, right now."

ON CITY EMPLOYEES WHO HAVE A "QUIT-AND-STAY MENTALITY."

"They quit a long time ago, but they come to work every single day."

A TEXTUAL CALL TO ARMS, TO CHIEF OF STAFF CHRISTINE.

"We have a job to do! This shit is hard. I made my choice for COS because I knew these times would come. I need you, boots on ready to roll. Me, Kwame! Fuck dem other MFs! What size boots you need nigga?"

*ON A SETTLEMENT OPPORTUNITY
IN 2004 IN THE WHISTLE-BLOWER
LAWSUIT, IN A TEXT TO A CITY LAWYER.*

"Reject that Bullshit.
FUCK THEM!"

Kwame and the Media (Part II)

*LEVELLING AN UNSUBSTANTIATED CHARGE
AT TV REPORTER NEMESIS STEVE WILSON.*

"Stop buying prostitutes, fat ass."

ON THE MEDIA.

"They're constantly, and I want
the public to see this, trying to
dismantle me in front of you."

ON THE MEDIA.

"I feel like, yeah, they finally got
me. But they got me because of
me. They got me because of me."

ON HIS STAR POWER.
"When I'm on the front page of the paper, they sell more papers than at any other time."

SHOUTING OUT A CAR WINDOW AT FREE PRESS REPORTERS WHO ACCURATELY WROTE THAT HE WAS GOING TO FIRE HIS SECURITY CHIEF.
"Hey, speculation writers!"

TO M.L. ELRICK, BEFORE A MEETING WITH THE FREE PRESS EDITORIAL BOARD, SEVERAL YEARS BEFORE THE TEXT MESSAGE SCANDAL BROKE.
"Boy I'd really like to hit you."

RALLYING SUPPORTERS BY LASHING OUT AT THE MEDIA.

"I don't believe that a Nielsen rating is worth the life of my children or your children."

ON THE MEDIA, DURING THE TEXT MESSAGE SCANDAL.

"This is ... the biggest story ever. I understand why you are following me with a camera. I understand why you're at my house. I understand why you've got to run your stories. Believe me, I do. I would run them if I was in the media."

The End

ON HIS RESIGNATION.

"To Whom It May Concern: I Kwame M. Kilpatrick resign from my position as Mayor of the City of Detroit effective September 18, 2008. With warm regards."

AFTER PLEADING GUILTY AND QUITTING HIS JOB.

"You done set me up for a comeback."

WAVING TO FAMILY AND FRIENDS AS HE WAS LED OFF TO JAIL.

"Y'all take it easy."

Kwame Kilpatrick

At 31, Kwame Malik Kilpatrick was the youngest man ever elected mayor of Detroit. A former college football standout, he may have also been the biggest chief executive in the city's 300-year history.

He took office in 2002 with great potential, big goals and insatiable appetites. The appetites would be his undoing.

By the time of his resignation in 2008, his potential was largely unrealized and his goals unfulfilled. Detroit had not become "the city God always intended it to be" and Kilpatrick, who often cited that divine objective for his hometown, had become the first sitting Detroit mayor in memory to be charged with a crime while in office.

In less than eight years after he burst onto the scene with his "Right here, right now" rallying cry, the man who had eschewed racial politics — until he really needed them — and who had pledged to never quit on Detroit, had moved with his wife and three sons into one of the richest, whitest suburbs in America.

In true Kilpatrick fashion, after telling the court he could only afford $6 a month in restitution toward the $1 million he agreed to repay Detroit for the text message scandal, he moved into a $1 million home in suburban Texas.

Kilpatrick's Life and Times

1970: Kwame Malik Kilpatrick born on June 8 to Carolyn Cheeks Kilpatrick and Bernard Kilpatrick, an ambitious and upwardly mobile political couple.

1984: Kilpatrick enters the most prestigious of Detroit's Public Schools — Cass Technical High School — where he meets Christine Rowland. While at Cass, she would meet one of Kilpatrick's childhood friends, Lou Beatty, whom she would later marry.

1992: Kilpatrick graduates from Florida A&M University in Tallahassee, where he was a captain of the football team and a standout offensive lineman.

1996: After working for several years as a teacher at the Marcus Garvey Academy in Detroit, Kilpatrick decides to run for his mother's seat in the state House after she becomes a candidate for Congress. Beatty helps run his campaign. Kilpatrick will serve three terms, during which he will campaign for Democrats across the state in hopes of winning their support in his bid to become Speaker of the House. But Republicans maintain their House majority, so Kilpatrick settles for Democratic Leader, becoming the first black to hold that position.

2001: Still relatively unknown outside his House district, Kilpatrick quietly puts together a coalition of political and business leaders and enters the

Detroit Mayor Kwame Kilpatrick tells
M.L. Elrick:

"Boy I'd really like to hit you,"

before meeting with the Free Press
editorial board. "That would only
result in another lawsuit against the
city," Elrick countered, to which Kilpatrick replied, "Yeah, you're probably
right."

race to replace out-going Mayor Dennis Archer. Just 30 years old — and only recently having removed his dental braces — he says meditation and a passage from the Bible signaled that his time had come. He later says he would have run even if Archer had sought a third term.

2002: According to local lore, Kilpatrick holds a wild party with strippers around Labor Day weekend in the mayoral residence, the Manoogian Mansion, which is unoccupied during renovations his family ordered. Descriptions of the party vary, but most accounts involve First Lady Carlita Kilpatrick showing up unannounced and assaulting a stripper. As the rumor swirls, Tamara Greene — a popular Detroit dancer known as Strawberry — is reputed to have danced for the mayor. Greene is murdered the following year. Despite many Detroiters' certainty the party happened, not one part of this widely-circulated story has been proven. Greene's killing remains unsolved.

2003: Kilpatrick, acting after Beatty says she received an anonymous note questioning Deputy Chief Gary Brown's trustworthiness, fires the veteran cop on May 9. Brown was head of the department's internal affairs bureau and was poised to investigate allegations of wrongdoing by members of the mayor's inner circle. He had also been told about the Manoogian Mansion party rumor. Brown files a whistle-blower lawsuit against Kilpatrick and the city. Brown alleges that Kilpatrick fired him because his planned investigation might have led to the discovery of the mayor's extramarital affairs. Harold Nelthrope and Walter Harris, police officers who worked as mayoral bodyguards, also file suit, alleging philandering and retaliation by the mayor. These lawsuits lead to subpoenas seeking Kilpatrick's and Beatty's text messages sent on city-issued devices.

2004: Kilpatrick and Beatty are deposed by the cops' attorney, Mike Stefani. Stefani protests what he deems are stall tactics when, at the end of the first deposition, Kilpatrick begins eating an apple as the session approaches its time limit. Stefani succeeds in gaining a second deposition session with Kilpatrick, at which the mayor denies affairs and says he ditches his police security so he can have time alone with the city he loves.

2005: Kilpatrick wins a stunning, last-minute, come-from-behind victory over challenger Freman Hendrix. Kilpatrick began the campaign with a radio commercial apologizing for his missteps, which included using city money to lease a Lincoln Navigator for his wife, profligate use of the city's credit card, and allegations of wild partying during out-of-town trips, all uncovered by the Detroit Free Press. Hendrix, who had served as Archer's deputy mayor, handily won the primary. Although Kilpatrick trailed in polls by as many as 19 points, he won the general election by several percentage points.

2007: After a raft of legal issues and disputes are resolved, Brown's and Nelthrope's whistle-blower case goes before a jury in August. After a few weeks of testimony, jurors deliberate for about an hour and award the cops $6.5 million in damages. Kilpatrick says he is "blown away" and vows to appeal. After rejecting entreaties that he settle the case, Kilpatrick abruptly reverses course on